D0532251

IF YOU WERE A...

Zookeeper

IF YOU WERE A...
Zookeeper

Virginia Schomp

BENCHMARK BOOKS

MARSHALL CAVENDISH
NEW YORK

Extra-long tongues help giraffes pluck leaves from high branches . . . and carrots from the zookeeper's hands.

If you were a zookeeper, you would watch over wild animals. You would keep them happy and healthy in their zoo homes.

An elephant trumpets—it's bathtime! Tigers roar—time to clean their swimming pool! Giraffes stamp their hooves for a tasty treat.

You would spend your day answering the wildest of calls, if you were a zookeeper.

A beluga whale's "kiss" brightens a zookeeper's day.

It's early morning. The zoo is not open to visitors yet. But the animals are stirring, and so are the zookeepers.

Keepers start their day with checkups. As they say good morning to each animal, they look closely to make sure it is well and content.

This keeper gives the elephants close-up care. At some zoos, keepers check on large or dangerous animals from a distance.

A hippo keeper rubs noses with a toothy friend.

Large zoos have many zookeepers. Each takes care of a different group of animals. The keepers get to know the personality of each animal in their care.

The hippopotamus keeper knows which hippos are gentle and which get cranky at mealtimes. To visitors, all the zoo's hippos may look alike. To their keeper, each is a one-of-a-kind wonder.

After morning checkups, keepers clean the animals' homes, or exhibits. They tidy up with shovels and brooms. They hose down rocks and floors. The zookeepers know that a clean exhibit helps keep zoo animals healthy and comfortable.

While one keeper sweeps up after an American alligator, another hoses down the aviary (AY-vee-er-ee)—the zoo birds' home.

Cleaning the zoo's giant fish tank is a soggy experience.

To a polar bear, a zoo iceberg is a cool place for napping.

In the past, zoo animals lived in small cages. Today many zoos have exhibits that copy the animals' natural homes. Trees, vines, and waterfalls become a tropical rain forest for crocodiles and colorful birds. Giant air-cooling machines and snowmakers re-create the polar bear's North Pole home.

Giraffes like looking for snacks high up, just as they would at home in the African grasslands.

It takes lots of hay to feed all the hungry mouths at the zoo.

In the wild, animals find their own meals. At the zoo, keepers work with nutrition experts to make sure each animal gets the food it likes and needs.

If you were a zookeeper, you might pick sunflowers for gorillas or bamboo stalks for giant pandas. You might lug in an elephant's feast—three hundred pounds of hay, grain, carrots, and apples.

To fix the birds' breakfast, you would chop up fruit, vegetables, raw fish, and frozen rats. The feed trays look scrumptious. But this is one salad bar where you won't want to nibble!

Each animal gets its own specially prepared meal.

A baby rhino enjoys a treat called browse—branches with leaves, twigs, and blossoms.

Zookeepers must know not only *what* to feed the animals but *when* and *how*. Some animals eat one big meal each day. Others need many small snacks.

If you cared for baboons or chimpanzees, you would hide raisins among the exhibit's rocks and trees. Searching

Leafy greens are part of the ostriches' carefully planned diet.

for treats keeps these curious creatures busy and alert.

To keep black bear cubs active, you might climb a tree and set out chunks of bread. The polar bear's favorite treat is a "fishsicle"—fish frozen inside a block of ice.

Tongues lick fur. Beaks smooth feathers. A soak in the swimming hole washes dirty hides clean. Most zoo animals groom themselves, but a few need the keeper's help to stay clean.

In the wild, elephants bathe in great rivers. At the zoo, you would use a hose and brush to give the giant beasts a showery scrub.

"Down!" you call, and the elephant drops to its knees. "Foot up!" It lifts its foot for a trim. Elephants and some other zoo animals are trained to follow commands so keepers and zoo doctors can give them the very best care.

Bathtime is fun for both keeper and elephant. Some zookeepers stand behind protective bars to give the big beasts their baths.

Helping baby gorillas grow up healthy is a fun part of the zoo doctor's job.

A lion licks a swollen paw. A fruit bat ignores a juicy grape. A bear cub isn't growing as fast as expected. Because keepers work so closely with zoo animals, they are usually the first to notice when one is hurt or sick. And when they spot any sign of trouble, they call the zoo's animal doctor, or veterinarian.

Tests tell the veterinarian what is wrong. The bat needs medicine. The bear needs vitamins. An operation will help the lion's injured paw to heal.

The "big cat" keepers and the veterinarian work together when a lion needs an operation.

Zoos used to buy new animals from hunters who captured them in the wild. Today most of the animals living in zoos were born there.

Because its mother could not take care of it, this baby gorilla lives in the zoo nursery.

At weigh-in time, baby hartebeests and black bear cubs can be a handful—or even a bucketful!

When a zoo baby is born, keepers call the veterinarian. If the baby is sick or weak, the doctor may send it to the zoo nursery. There the newborn is kept well fed, cozy, and safe. Keepers weigh it every day to make sure it is growing properly.

A nursery keeper and a young lowland gorilla share a special bond.

This sandhill crane chick is fed with a hand puppet so it won't become more comfortable with people than with other birds.

A crane chick raised in the zoo nursery may have trouble getting along with other cranes. It is so used to people it doesn't know how to behave around birds.

To solve this problem, zoos try to keep mothers and babies together. But if a newborn must be taken to the nursery, keepers raise it with creatures of its own kind. As soon as it is old enough, the youngster returns to live with its zoo family.

In the zoo, a zebra mother and her foal are safe from hunters and other dangers.

Every zoo birth is good news. But zookeepers are especially happy when the new baby belongs to an endangered species.

An endangered species is a kind of animal that is in danger of dying out completely. People have destroyed the rain forests or other wild places the animal needs to survive.

Today zoos are working to save endangered species. Like a modern-day Noah's ark, the zoo gives animals a safe place to live and raise families. Sometimes, when a new home outside the zoo is found, endangered animals born in the zoo are set free in the wild.

Destruction of Asian rain forests has taken away this baby orangutan's natural home.

A tree kangaroo is the guest of honor at a zookeeper training class.

Are you strong enough to haul a hippo's supper? Are you patient enough to teach a zoo-born monkey how to peel a banana? Would you like to take care of zoo animals?

To become a zookeeper, you must study animal science in college. Then you may work as an intern— a student who trains with experienced keepers.

You'll find that the zookeeper's job is hard, messy, and sometimes dangerous. It is also fun and full of surprises. The best part is knowing that your work keeps wild animals safe and happy in their zoo homes.

A keeper intern makes friends with a baby hippo.

ZOO ANIMALS IN TIME

In ancient times, rulers collected wild animals to show off their own power and importance. The ancient Romans forced prisoners to fight to the death against hungry lions.

Emperor Akbar of the Mogul Empire inspects a captured elephant. Specially trained veterinarians cared for the animals at the public zoos that Akbar set up all across India in the late 1500s.

Until recent times, zoo animals lived a sad life behind bars.

A ZOOKEEPER'S CLOTHING AND TOOLS

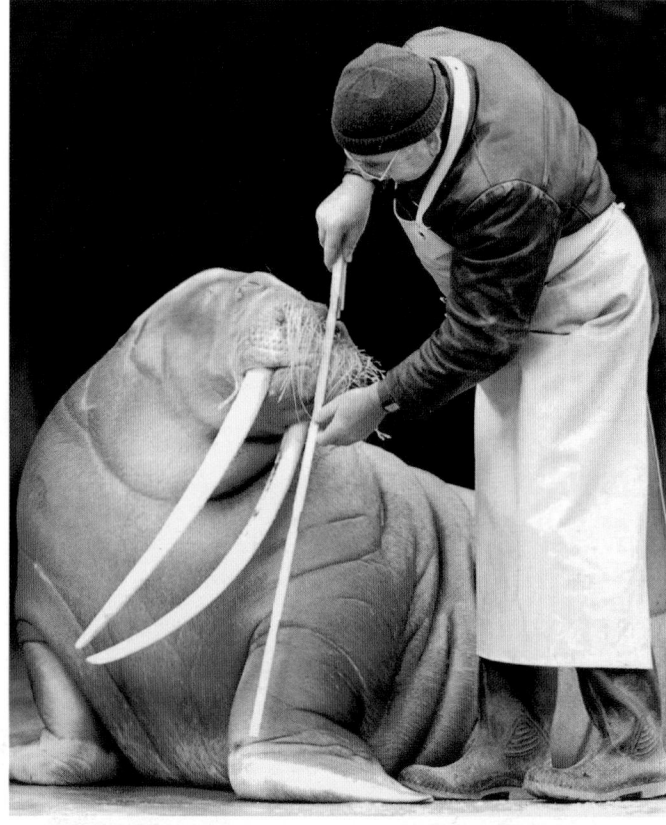

An apron and boots help keep clothes clean.

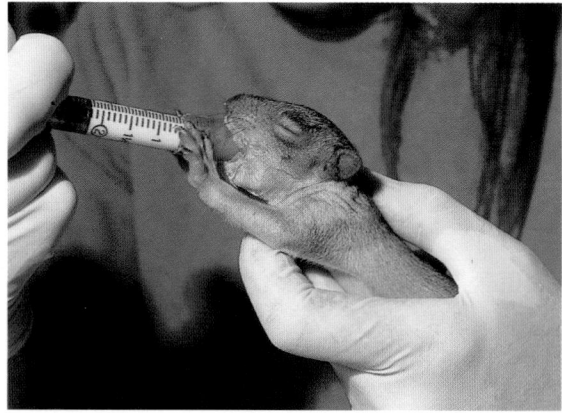

eyedropper—for feeding baby animals

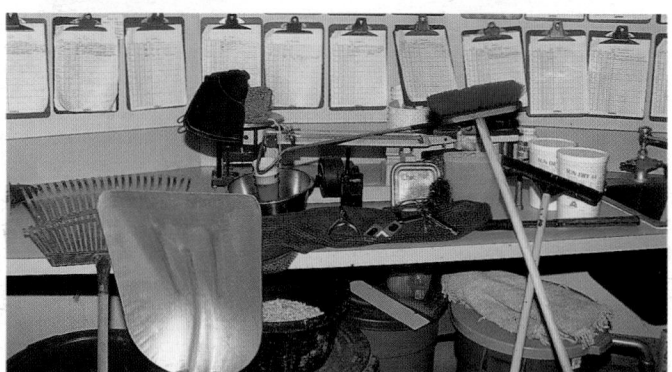

rake, shovel, broom, food containers, snake hook, nail clippers, charts

scale—for weighing eggs or small animals

WORDS TO KNOW

"big cats" Lions, tigers, leopards, and jaguars. The "big cats" are the cat family's best hunters and the only cats that can roar.

endangered species A kind of animal that was once very common but is now rare and in danger of dying out completely.

exhibit The part of the zoo where an animal lives and can be seen by visitors.

intern A student who gets an on-the-job education by working alongside someone who has more experience.

nutrition The food an animal needs to live and grow.

rain forest A type of forest that receives a large amount of rain year-round and is rich in plant and animal life.

veterinarian A doctor who takes care of the health of animals.

*This book is for Jessica and Kristin,
our precocious Pocono pianists*

Benchmark Books
Marshall Cavendish Corporation
99 White Plains Road
Tarrytown, New York 10591
Copyright © 2000 by Marshall Cavendish Corporation

Library of Congress Cataloging-in-Publication Data
Schomp, Virginia, date
If you were a—zookeeper / Virginia Schomp.
p.   cm.   Includes index.
Summary: Describes the work of zookeepers and includes a brief history of zoos.
ISBN 0-7614-0918-1
1. Zoo keepers—Juvenile literature. [1. Zoo keepers. 2. Zoos. 3. Occupations.] I. Title.
QL50.5.S375   2000   636.088'9'023—dc21   98-34701   CIP   AC

Photo research by Rose Corbett Gordon

Front cover:courtesy of *Tom Stack & Associates*:Tom & Therisa Stack.
Index Stock Imagery:Tom McCarthy,1; H. Horenstein,31.*Wildlife Conservation Society, headquartered at the Bronx Zoo:*
2,4,6,8(right),12,18,22,19,30(top right); Diane Shapiro,9(left),15; Dennis DeMello,16,19,21(left),27;Bill Meng,30(bottom right).
Archive Photos/Reuters: Megan Lewis,5(right),24; Benoit Doppagne,7;Joe Traver,10(left);Reinhard Krause,20;Peter Mueller,30(top left).
*Earth Scenes:*Zig Leszczynski,8(left); *Animals, Animals:* Miriam Agnon,11. *Tom Stack & Associates:*Tom & Therisa Stack,13;Brian Parker,25.
*Peter Arnold, Inc.:*Michael Fairchild,14;Lynn Rogers,21(right); Carl R. Sams II,23. *Zoological Society of San Diego.* 26,30(bottom left).
*North Wind Picture Archives:*29(top left). *Art Resource,NY:*Victoria & Albert Museum,London,28(bottom right).

Printed in Hong Kong
1   3   5   7   8   6   4   2

INDEX